Copyright © 2020 Terri Whitaker

No part of this book may be reproduced in any form or by any means, graphic, electronic, or mechanical, including photocopying, recording, taping or by any information storage retrieval system, without the written permission of the copyright holder.

The right of Terri Whitaker to be identified as the author of this work has been asserted in accordance with the Copyright, Designs and Patents Act 1988 sections 77 and 78.

Cover photograph © James Whitaker. All rights reserved.

Cover design by Mark Whitaker.

Contents

Acknowledgments 9
Advice 11
Belief 12
Blind to Goodness 13
Commitment 14
Communication 15
Compassion 16
Complacency 17
Criticism 18
Differences 19
Difficulties 20
Equality 21
Estranged from God 22
Faith 23
Fear 24
Forgiveness 25
Freedom 26
Gentleness 27
God's Forgiveness 28
God's Help 29
God's Love 30
Goodness 31
Gratitude 32
Greed 33
Helping Others 34
Hope 35
Humility 36
I Am With You Always 37
Jealousy 38

Judging Others	39
Keeping in Touch	40
Kingdom of God	41
Lead, Kindly Light	42
Light of the World	44
Listening	45
Living Life to the Full	46
Losing Your Life	47
Love	48
Love One Another	49
Love Your Enemies	50
Making Choices	51
Making Demands on God	52
Money	53
Neighbourliness	54
Not Ours to Keep	55
Patience	56
Peacemakers	57
Perseverance	58
Poor in Spirit	59
Prayer	60
Preaching	61
Prejudice	62
Pride	63
Priorities	64
Problems	65
Rejection	66
Retribution	67
Road to Life	68
Seek and You Will Find	69
Seek First The Kingdom of God	70
Selflessness	71
Sharing	72
Sincerity	73

Spirit of Life	74
Spiritual Maturity	75
Suffering	76
Superiority	77
Talents	78
Temptation	79
The Good Shepherd	80
Tolerance	81
Trust in God	82
Unity	83
Wisdom	84
Worry	85
Worthiness	86
Wrongdoing	87
Christmas	88
The Light of the World	88
A Christmas Carol	89
Shepherds and Magi	90
Post-Christmas	91
New Year	92
New Wineskins	92
Resoluteness	93
Epiphany	94
Gifts	94
Spiritual Journey	95
Valentine's Day	96
St David's Day	97
St Patrick's Day	98
St George's Day	99
Shrove Tuesday	100
Lent	101
Change of Heart	101
Forty Days	102
Temptation	103

Prayer	104
Mothering Sunday	105
Palm Sunday	106
Maundy Thursday	107
Good Friday	108
Easter Day	109
Pentecost	110
Ascension Day	111
Guy Fawkes Night	112
Remembrance Day	113
Let Them be One	113
Lay Down His Life	114
BBC's Children In Need	115
Index	117

Acknowledgments

I would like to thank my good friend, Noelle Duffy, without whose encouragement I would not have attempted this venture.

I would also like to thank my son, Mark, for his loving and patient proof-reading, editing, suggestions and technical expertise, without which this book would not have got off the ground.

Advice

We've probably all met Job's Comforters – people who tell us they're trying to help, but leave us feeling worse instead of better. So it is in the Book of Job.

Although the advice offered by Job's three friends is well-intentioned, they seem to think they have reasoned everything out and have all the answers. They tend to lecture him in an academic way that offers little comfort, getting increasingly annoyed with him when he refuses to see things their way.

Job's fourth visitor has a different approach. He is younger than the others and has held back, thinking his lack of experience and learning renders him less wise than the others, but now realises that it is God's Spirit in a person that makes them wise. He is much warmer; he addresses Job by name, which the others don't, and he speaks from his heart. His speech is full of God's goodness. It is only after this speech that Job hears the voice of God and all his problems disappear.

This story reminds us that no matter how insightful we may be, we don't really understand the full nature of our friends' problems. Therefore, help, no matter how simple, that comes from a heart full of God's love, is much better than a cold expert opinion.

Belief

'Seeing is believing' is a familiar saying, but Jesus turned this into 'believing is seeing'. It is only when we believe that we truly see.

John 20:24 tells us that the apostle, who has become known as Doubting Thomas, refused to believe until he had seen. Jesus said, 'Blessed are those who have not seen and yet have believed.'

Mark 10:46 tells of a blind man, Bartimaeus, who called out to Jesus to have mercy on him. 'What do you want me to do for you?' Jesus asked him. Bartimaeus said, 'I want to see.' Jesus said, 'Your faith has healed you.' Immediately Bartimaeus received his sight.

If we try to follow the teachings of Jesus, no matter how difficult, or even impossible they seem, we will be cured of our selfishness, our lack of forgiveness; we'll feel much better, and we'll see a change occur in our life. If we want a better life, we first have to believe – have faith – that the teachings of Jesus can help us. We then have to put those teachings into practise by trusting in God, caring about others and being selfless. Only then will we start to see clearly.

Blind to Goodness

Luke 24:13 tells of two followers of Jesus walking seven miles from Jerusalem to Emmaus after the crucifixion. Jesus joined them, but they didn't recognise him. They spent all that time together, walking and talking, but it was not until he broke bread with them that 'their eyes were opened and they recognised him, and he disappeared from their sight. They asked each other, "Were not our hearts burning within us while he talked with us?"'

How often are we blind to the presence of Jesus? How often are we blind to the presence of a good person? We can sometimes spend a long time – maybe years – with a good person and not truly recognise their goodness, until they've gone. Only then do we remember how good they made us feel when we were with them. Every time we encounter a good person – be they a stranger, or someone so familiar that we take them for granted – we are in the presence of Jesus, because God is love.

Jesus said that every time we do a kind act for someone, we are doing it for him (Matthew 25:35). Let's not be too blind to recognise that.

Commitment

Matthew 19:16 (Mark 10:17; Luke 18:18) tells of a man who asked Jesus what he must do to get eternal life. Jesus replied that he must obey the commandments. The man says he has kept all the commandments, what more can he do. Jesus says, 'Sell your possessions and give to the poor, then follow me.' When the young man heard this, he went away sad, because he had great wealth.

This story is not about money, but about how much we are prepared to commit ourselves to God. Being rich is not wrong (Abraham was rich), but caring more about money than we care about God and our neighbour is wrong. To have a good and lasting relationship with anyone requires mutual unconditional love. If we are prepared to do only so much, our relationship is not going to last. The same applies to our relationship with God. He loves us more than anyone else could begin to love us. We are his precious children. Would he do anything harmful to us? He wants a better life, not a worse life, for us. We have to put our fears behind us and commit ourselves unconditionally.

Communication

A breakdown in communications can be frustrating. If it happens between friends and family it can be heartbreaking.

In the story of the Tower of Babel (Genesis 1:11), the people had become too full of their own importance, so God confused their language and they were unable to communicate – they babbled.

The day of Pentecost (Acts 2) reversed this situation. The Spirit of God came down on people from different nations, who had come together to celebrate the Feast of Pentecost, and suddenly the language barrier was overcome – all these strangers could understand what was being said.

If we find that communication has broken down between ourselves and others – friends, family members, neighbours, or colleagues – maybe we need to ask ourselves if we have started to rely too much on our own ingenuity and pushed God out. God understands our problems better than we do, and we need to listen to him; we also need to listen with love to what others have to say. Only when the Spirit of God is welcomed in will we start to listen clearly, understand clearly and thus communicate.

Compassion

Jesus had great compassion for everyone regardless of their status, and he considered everyone to be his brothers and sisters. He said: 'Whatever you did for one of the least of these brothers of mine, you did for me' (Matthew 25:40).

He was constantly encouraging people to change from an unloving way of thinking and acting to having compassion and concern for others.

Just as it grieves loving parents to see their children bickering and fighting and being unkind to one another, so it grieves God when we are unkind to one another. Just as loving parents want to see their children being kind to each other, helping each other and caring about each other, so too, God's wish is for us to care about each other.

If we can try to remember this always and therefore put that little extra effort into being helpful, kind and caring at all times to everyone, regardless of who they are, we will be doing God's will and making the world a happier place.

Complacency

'At least I'm not as bad as him/her.' How often have we comforted ourselves with these words? So long as we can find somebody worse than ourselves, we can feel smug.

Jesus told a parable about a Pharisee and a tax collector who went to the temple to pray (Luke 18:9). Pharisees strictly observed Jewish tradition by fasting and giving alms, and maybe had good reason to believe themselves better than average. On the other hand, tax collectors were hated because they worked for the Romans, collecting taxes, and they ran something rather like a protection racket to extort more than the Romans had levied.

In the parable, the Pharisee thanks God that he's not like other bad people, while the tax collector humbly says, 'God, have mercy on me, a sinner'. Jesus said it was the tax collector, not the Pharisee, who would get closer to God, because he who exalts himself will be humbled and he who humbles himself will be exalted.

We shouldn't compare ourselves with people we think are less good than us, but should acknowledge our own faults and strive to overcome them; this way we'll avoid complacency and make ourselves better people.

Criticism

People who go on television shows such as Strictly Come Dancing or The X Factor have to be prepared to take a lot of criticism. Most of us could not bear such public humiliation. Most of us cannot bear private criticism either. However, if we want to improve ourselves we have to accept, not just praise when we do something right, but also criticism when we do something wrong.

Jesus said: 'If your brother does something wrong, go and show him his fault, just between the two of you. If he listens to you, you have won your brother over.' (Matthew 18:15)

If we find fault with someone, we should offer criticism out of love and a sincere wish to help. We do not help someone by criticising them behind their back, nor do we help someone by letting rip and pointing out their faults simply to get something off our chest and make ourselves feel better. Only by asking God to fill our hearts with love for the person at fault and approaching that person with total love, humility and compassion will we stand a chance of them listening to us, helping them, and therefore winning them over.

Differences

'Why Can't a Woman be More Like a Man?' sings the somewhat pompous Professor Henry Higgins in My Fair Lady.

Indeed, we constantly criticise people for not being more like ourselves. We find it difficult to be tolerant of what we see as other people's weaknesses, compared with our strengths.

In 1 Corinthians 12, Paul tried to explain to people who thought they were better than others that we may all be different, but we are not better or worse than each other. He pointed out that it is because of our differences that we need each other. He used, as an example, the body which is one unit, but has many parts and he explained that we need each different part of our body. If the whole body were an eye, where would be the sense of hearing, he asks; or if it were an ear, where would be the sense of smell? The hand is no more important than the foot. They are different, but equally important for the functions they perform.

Just as Professor Higgins learns to love Eliza Doolittle because she is so different from him, so we too must learn to love people who are different from us.

Difficulties

When Jesus spoke of taking up a cross and following him (Matthew 16:24; Mark 8:34; Luke 9:23), he was emphasising how difficult it is to follow his teachings.

It is always easier to do the wrong thing, than it is to do the right thing. It is much easier to hate your enemy, than to love him. It is much easier to hold a grudge, than to forgive. It is much easier to see the faults in others, than to see our own faults. It is much easier to be prejudiced against people who are different from us, than it is to see them as our equal.

We constantly need God's help in order to do the right thing, and even then it's difficult. Why bother? Why struggle to do the right thing when doing the wrong thing is so much easier?

Funnily enough, the nicest people we know – the ones who aren't selfish or self-centred; who are the best company because they always have a ready smile and a good sense of humour; are good listeners and seldom complain or criticise; who seem to be blessed with a happy and carefree life – are the ones who, every day, carry that invisible cross.

Equality

In Shakespeare's The Winter's Tale a young shepherdess and a prince fall in love. The shepherdess knows that the difference between her status and that of the prince makes their situation hopeless. She points out the unfairness of this when she says that the same sun than shines upon his Royal court also shines on her humble cottage.

We can apply this reasoning to God's love, which falls on the rich and poor alike. It is we humans who differentiate between rich and poor people, or between well-educated and poorly-educated people, or between beautiful and plain people, or between gifted and less-gifted people. God, like any loving parent, loves all his children in equal measure. It's up to us as to how we respond to that love.

In The Winter's Tale the shepherdess discovers that she is, in fact, the beloved daughter of a king, so is an equal to the prince. When we realise that we are a beloved child of God, we can appreciate that, regardless of our status in this world, we are equal to all others.

Estranged from God

In the Parable of the Lost Son (Luke 15:11) the son asks for his share of his father's estate in advance of his father's death, which is almost like wishing his father dead. He then leaves home for a distant country and blows all his money on wild living. Penniless and starving, he remembers his father, so returns home.

The story says that while the son was still a long way off, his father saw him, ran to him, clasped him in his arms and kissed him. The fact that the father saw him while he was still a long way off suggests that, while the son forgot about his father, the father never forgot about his son and looked out for him every day, hoping for his return.

Most of us are guilty, at some time, of forgetting about our heavenly father, but he never stops hoping for our return. We return when we realize that – despite having everything money can buy – we are spiritually starved and impoverished when we are estranged from our heavenly father. That is what causes our craving for something more, our sense of something missing. It is only by returning to our heavenly father will we find the happiness we seek.

Faith

Practice makes perfect. This applies to most things in life – sports training springs immediately to mind. It can also apply to faith.

Some people don't like the God of the Old Testament – they say he's always 'testing' people. However, we could think of it as encouraging us to perfect our faith. Just as a professional coach will not push his students beyond their capabilities, but will concentrate on trying to strengthen their weaknesses, so too God will not expect from us more than we can give as we wrestle with the weaker parts of our faith. Whether we are at the tentative testing-the-water stage or the going-for-gold stage in our faith, God will urge us on to push ourselves that extra bit, to take that leap of faith, to trust.

Abraham is considered a man of great faith, but his faith fell short a couple of times when he lied about his wife being his sister because he didn't trust that God would look after them. However, after a lifetime of discovering that no matter how far God pushed him, God never let him down, Abraham's faith reached perfection when he was prepared to sacrifice his precious, long-awaited son, if that was what God wanted (Genesis 12-22).

Fear

Fear is a terrible thing. We have only to remind ourselves of the times our fears have proved unfounded to know that fear is something we should not submit to.

Matthew 14:22 (and Mark 6:45; John 6:16) tells us that when the disciples saw Jesus walking on the sea, they cried out in fear, but Jesus called to them: 'Courage! It's me! Don't be afraid.' When Jesus said 'Come', Peter got out of the boat and started walking towards Jesus, but then took fright and began to sink. Jesus saved him, but was disappointed at Peter's lack of faith.

Obviously, this story is not persuading us to attempt walking across the Mersey! It is, however, encouraging us to have faith. God loves each and every one of us and doesn't want any of us to feel afraid. God is always there for us. We mustn't allow ourselves to drown under a sea of fear, but rather trust in God's love, knowing that God, not fear, will save us.

Forgiveness

Jesus told the Parable of the Unforgiving Debtor (Matthew 18:23) in response to Peter's question of how many times should we forgive someone who keeps offending us.

The parable tells of a servant who owed his master the huge debt of 10,000 talents, but his master took pity on him and cancelled the debt. However, this same servant took no pity on someone who owed him the tiny (by comparison) sum of 100 denarii (6,000 denarii equalled one talent). This made the master very angry.

The message of this parable is that God loves and takes pity on us and in turn we should radiate that love and forgiveness to others. The amount of love and forgiveness that God bestows on us is so huge it is beyond imagining, compared with the tiny amount of love and forgiveness that we should give to others.

Being unforgiving actually makes us feel miserable, because it distances us from God. When we forgive, we experience a happiness that comes from being close to God.

Freedom

In John's first letter he says, 'God is love. Whoever lives in love lives in God, and God in him. There is no fear in love. Perfect love drives out fear, because fear has to do with punishment. The one who fears is not made perfect in love' (1 John 4:16).

The theologian, Bernard Häring, argues that in almost all religions there is still a temptation to use the potent motive of fear, forcing people to toe the line in religion and other things. It is a satanic notion, he says, to exploit the name of God and Christ to make people submissive through feelings of anxiety, even if this exploitation is for noble causes. He believes that neurotic anxiety, injected through teaching, structures, and behaviour, along with associated fearful expectations, all too often block the way to true freedom. Being caught up in fear of a terrifying, menacing God stifles us; it throttles the healing and liberating energies of openness. He believes that many hostilities and even the cruellest wars have been at least partly caused by sick fear, anxiety and mistrust.

Only love frees us from the paralysis of fear and frees us to trust.

Gentleness

There is an Aesop Fable about the Wind and the Sun who were disputing which was the stronger. They saw a traveller coming down the road and decided that whichever of them could cause the traveller to take off his cloak would be regarded as the stronger. The Sun retired behind a cloud and the Wind began to blow as hard as he could upon the traveller, but the harder he blew the more closely did the traveller wrap his cloak round him. At last the Wind had to give up in despair. Then the Sun came out and shone in all his glory upon the traveller, who soon found it too hot to walk with his cloak on.

In 1 Kings 19:11 it says that the Lord was not in windstorm, earthquake, nor fire, but in a gentle whisper. Mark 4:35 tells us that Jesus rebuked the wind and it was calm.

Like the Sun in the Aesop Fable, God is not a forceful bully. If we want to be a strong influence for good, we should strive to be gentle and calm for, as the Fable shows, gentleness has a stronger effect than severity.

God's Forgiveness

The Parable of the Prodigal Son (Luke 15:11) teaches about God's infinite love. On his father's death, the son would have inherited a share of his father's estate, but by asking for it in advance, it's almost like wishing his father dead. However, his father gives it to him. He leaves home for a distant country and blows the lot on wild living. Only after falling as low as possible does he think of the one person who will help him, so returns to his father.

While he was still a long way off, his father saw him and was moved with pity. He ran to the boy, clasped him in his arms and kissed him. A father kissing a son was not the done thing at that time, so this emphasizes how overjoyed the father was. Regardless of how much the son had hurt his father's feelings and despite the fact that he'd gone far away, probably not giving a thought for his father, his father was waiting for him, ready to forgive and forget.

No matter how many wrongs we may have done, or how far we may have distanced ourselves from God, he still loves us and is eagerly awaiting our return.

God's Help

There's a saying: 'God helps those who help themselves'. In a way this is true. Like any loving parent, God supports us when we make an effort. On the other hand, however, a loving parent would not want to help a child who wanted to achieve something purely for self-seeking motives, pushing aside his brothers and sisters in the process. But a loving parent would want to help a child who was putting an effort in to helping his brothers and sisters.

We are told in 1 Kings 3 that when Solomon was made king and given the opportunity to ask God for whatever he wanted, his request was not a selfish one. He didn't ask for long life or wealth, but asked for a discerning heart to govern God's people and to distinguish between right and wrong. God was very pleased with him and gave him a wise and discerning heart, which is how Solomon became the wisest person ever known.

God will always help us, provided our motives are good. We just need to make sure that we are wanting to do the right thing for the right reasons.

God's Love

'And God saw that it was good.' This phrase is repeated seven times in the first chapter of the Bible (Genesis 1). Regardless of whether or not we read the story of Creation literally, the message that comes across is that of a loving parent creating a beautiful world for his children to inhabit. Any expectant-parent who has transformed their dingy spare bedroom into a bright and colourful nursery can relate to this.

Parents also know how children sometimes experience difficulty in understanding why they can't have what they want and why they have to do things they don't want to. Likewise, we sometimes have difficulty understanding why God seems to prevent things turning out the way we would like. One thing we can be sure of: just as any loving parent wants only what is good for their child – so too does God.

Goodness

'The salt of the earth' is how we describe a good person. Jesus told his disciples: 'You are the salt of the earth' (Matthew 5:13). He was telling them that just as salt is used for making food taste better, so too the followers of Jesus should behave in such a way as to make life better for people. Salt is also used for preserving and, so too, Christians should behave in a way that helps keep people good and saves them from turning bad.

It's easy to fall into the trap of being concerned only with making life better for ourselves, or only helping in a situation that will benefit us. That is not the example that Jesus set. From time to time we should ask ourselves if we are behaving in a way that makes life better for other people, or if we are too wrapped up in ourselves to care; also if we are behaving in a way that helps other people to lead a good life, or if we are encouraging wrong actions. In other words, are we being the salt of the earth.

Gratitude

'Thank God!' we often exclaim. But how often do we truly thank God?

Luke 17:11 tells of ten men who had leprosy and asked Jesus to take pity on them. He healed them all, but only one returned to thank him and praise God. To this one Jesus said, 'Your faith has made you well', indicating that although they had all been physically healed, this one received the bonus of spiritual health.

We all receive gifts from God every day in hundreds of little ways, but they are so much a part of our life that we often take them for granted. How many of us remember to say thank you? Those who take the many gifts of food, family, friendships, etc., for granted and never think to thank God for what they have, are easily made discontent about what they haven't got. But those who receive these same gifts and remember to thank God for what they have, are given the extra gift of contentment and that feeling of spiritual wellbeing that shines out.

Greed

Jesus said: 'Watch out! Be on your guard against all kinds of greed; a man's life does not consist in the abundance of his possessions' (Luke 12:15).

Bernard de Mandeville, (1670-1733), philosopher, political economist and satirist, who became infamous for his publication The Fable of the Bees, maintained that the economy flourishes if people desire as much as possible. Greed is good because it increases consumption and so develops the market. The consumer society encourages limitless desire, and its typical addiction is shopping. The challenge for consumerism is to make us go on desiring, never satisfied, always needing more. Advertisements are always informing us of new desires that we never knew we had, manufacturing desire, so that our consumption is endless

Margaret Atkins, newspaper columnist and theologian wrote: 'Advertising aims to break the link between goods and their real purpose: the car is no longer for getting to work, but rather for attracting nubile young women, or racing across empty deserts, or making your peers jealous. Our defence against the system is to keep asking ourselves, "What is this really for?"' We need to be aware at all times of the difference between 'need' and 'greed'.

Helping Others

The book of Esther is about a girl who, because of her beauty, is taken for a wife by the King of Persia, but does not reveal that she is Jewish. The time comes when the King is going to condemn all Jews to death. Esther is asked to plead for mercy on their behalf. She agrees, even though it means possible death for her also.

The important message that comes out of Esther is that if you find yourself in a position of influence or power, you should use it for the good of others and not simply to benefit yourself.

Phrases like, 'My hands are tied', 'It's out of my hands', 'There's nothing I can do about it', slip easily from the tongue when we think that someone else's problem is not our problem. But, if we view everyone as our brother or sister, we should do our utmost to help them. Fear of the consequences to ourselves can prevent us from even trying to help. On those occasions we can remember that Esther's belief that she's in the position she is 'for such a time as this' (4:14), results in the safe delivery of Esther and her people.

Hope

'If only I'd known then what I know now!' How often do we hear this?

In the Parable of the Sower (Matthew 13:1; Mark 4:1; Luke 8:1) Jesus gives four examples of the way we react to the opportunity of living a good life. Some reject it outright. Some welcome it enthusiastically, but, lacking deep conviction, give up at the first difficulty. Some grasp it and hold on, but then allow themselves to be overwhelmed by negative thoughts that strangle their strength of belief. Finally, there are those who embrace the opportunity and tenaciously hold fast to it, growing stronger all the time.

This story does not apply only to different types of people, but also to different stages in life. If we have sadly watched loved ones pass up opportunity after opportunity to change their way of life, this parable offers the hope that they may reach the stage when they will seize the opportunity and not let it go. Then we can thank God that they know now what we knew then.

Humility

Jesus said: 'Whoever humbles himself will be exalted' (Matthew 23:12). But what exactly is humility?

It's obviously not the insincere grovelling of the odious Uriah Heep in David Copperfield who pretends to be subservient by repeating 'I'm ever so 'umble'. It's not passively accepting bad things that happen – this can be apathy and inaction rather than humility. It's not necessarily quiet or introverted behaviour – this can be a character trait of timid people. It's not being a door-mat – this is humiliation and shouldn't be encouraged. It's not feeling worthless, because in the sight of God we are very precious.

Humility doesn't come naturally, but has to be consciously developed by not constantly wanting our own way; by not wanting to be in charge all the time; by being aware of our own faults instead of complaining about the faults of others.

The word 'humility' comes from the Latin word humus meaning 'earth' and connects to the word 'human'. Therefore, to be humble is to be down to earth; to be realistic and honest; to know that we are no better than any other human, and not to arrogantly exalt ourselves.

I Am With You Always

Jesus said: 'I am with you always; yes, to the end of time' (Matthew 28:20). These words have proved true indeed. Why is it that a mere carpenter, who grew up in a place from where nothing good could come (John 1:46) and who died the death of a common criminal, still inspires, worldwide, after 2,000 years?

There may be many parts of the Bible that are no longer applicable in this modern age, such as Paul's insistence that 'if a woman does not cover her head, she should have her hair cut off' (1 Corinthians 11:6).

However, the words of Jesus are as relevant today as they were 2,000 years ago – they are timeless. He taught us to love one another (Matthew 5:43; 19:19; 22:37; Mark 12:30; Luke 6:27; 10:27; John 13:34; 15:12); to forgive 'not seven times, but seventy-seven times' (Matthew 18:22); to turn the other cheek (Luke 6:29); to trust in God and not worry because worrying is futile, it cannot change anything (Matthew 6:25).

It is as important today as it was 2,000 years ago that we try to follow these teachings if we want to live a good life and find inner peace.

Jealousy

Jealousy – 'the green-eyed monster' in Shakespeare's Othello – is a terrible thing. It drives Othello to commit murder.

There's jealousy and resentment in the Parable of the Lost Son (Luke 15:11). When the elder son finds that his father is celebrating the return of the younger son, he says angrily: 'All these years I have slaved for you and never once disobeyed any orders of yours, yet you never offered me so much as a kid for me to celebrate with my friends. But, when this son of yours returns after spending all your money, you kill the fatted calf.'

Actually, most of us would react as the elder son reacts and feel justified in doing so. But regardless of how we may justify feelings of jealousy and resentment, they are wrong; they should never be accepted as being right and should be fought against. It's easier to give in to feelings of jealousy than to fight against them, but if the elder son had overcome his jealousy he could have shared in his father's happiness.

Giving in to jealousy can lead to tragic unhappiness, as Othello discovers.

Judging Others

There is a saying that goes: 'When you point the finger, remember there are three other fingers pointing back at you.' This is a reminder when we are critical of others that we may have far more faults than them. We can always see other people's faults easier than we can see our own.

Jesus said: 'Why do you look at the speck of sawdust in your brother's eye and pay no attention to the plank in your own eye?' (Matthew 7:3; Luke 6:41). By paying no attention to our own faults, we are being hypocritical if we criticize other people's faults. Therefore, Jesus is speaking about hypocrisy rather than judgment itself. Where people are acting in an evil manner, it is right that we should condemn their behaviour. Jesus does not call on us to accept any behaviour, or to refrain from judgment altogether. What he warns us about is self-righteous judgment. We should always look at our own actions and motives with as critical an eye as we are keen to turn on others. As Jesus said: 'Take the log out of your own eye first, and then you will see clearly enough to take the splinter out of your brother's eye.'

Keeping in Touch

'Out of sight, out of mind' is a very true saying. We all know how easy it is to forget about those we don't see regularly. So, how do we keep in mind God, who we never see? Well, just as we can forget about those we don't care about, we never forget about those we do care about. If our loved ones are away from home we can send them long letters, maybe unburdening all our worries, maybe asking for their advice, maybe telling them how much we appreciate their support, maybe telling them how much we love them. We can also send shorter messages, maybe more frequently, via e-mail. Or we can send text messages. With text messages we can send several per day, that can consist of just a few words, maybe a quick cry for help, or a word of thanks.

God likes to hear from us as much as we like to hear from those we love. So if we want to keep in touch with the one who truly loves us and wants to help us more than anyone else we know, we need to get texting, e-mailing and writing – and be alert to replies.

Kingdom of God

'Another Place' on Crosby beach is a creation of the artist, Antony Gormley. He said that the idea for his hundred iron men, all facing towards the horizon, came about when he started thinking about departure, and to reflecting that when things get tough our thoughts turn to somewhere else. He thought about the exodus of immigrants to the New World, and the journeys that all of us make when we go on holiday. We all dream of the Promised Land, he said.

Certainly, if our circumstances are making us unhappy, we can alleviate our unhappiness by moving to another place. However, if our unhappiness is caused by something within ourselves, no amount of moving will solve our problem in the long term, for we take ourselves with us wherever we go.

Jesus said: 'The kingdom of God is within you' (Luke 17:21). This indicates that the kingdom is spiritual and internal, rather than physical and external, meaning that the closer we come to God by following the teaching of Christ, the more we will experience the joy and inner peace of the paradise we all seek.

Lead, Kindly Light

In the summer of 1833 the famous Christian, John Henry Newman, made a trip to Europe, but the return journey proved long and arduous. He fell ill with a fever and was thought to be dying. He recovered, but spent weeks waiting for a boat and subsequently was becalmed at sea off the coast of Sardinia. It was during this time of feeling homesick and weak, on 16th June, that he wrote a poem, which became the well-known hymn, Lead, Kindly Light.

Newman was a fiercely independent-minded and intellectually gifted man, but in this poem he is saying that he is glad to put aside all his own reasoning and doubts. The words: 'I do not ask to see the distant scene; one step is enough for me' shows that he is entrusting his entire being and future to the wisdom of God. He admits that he was not always like this: 'I loved to choose and see my path; but now lead Thou me on'. He also confesses that: 'Pride ruled my will.'

When we are feeling worried about our future, we too need to put aside our doubts and put our complete trust in God.

Lead, Kindly Light, amidst th'encircling gloom,
  Lead Thou me on!
The night is dark, and I am far from home,
  Lead Thou me on!
Keep Thou my feet; I do not ask to see
  The distant scene; one step enough for me.

I was not ever thus, nor prayed that Thou
  Shouldst lead me on;
I loved to choose and see my path; but now
  Lead Thou me on!
I loved the garish day, and, spite of fears,
  Pride ruled my will. Remember not past years!

So long Thy power hath blest me, sure it still
  Will lead me on.
O'er moor and fen, o'er crag and torrent, till
  The night is gone,
And with the morn those angel faces smile,
  Which I have loved long since, and lost awhile!

Lead, Kindly Light
John Henry Newman

Light of the World

Somebody made the point that when we walk towards a light our shadow is behind us and all we see is the light, but when we turn our back to the light and walk away from it, all we see is our own shadow.

Jesus said: 'I am the light of the world. Whoever follows me will never walk in darkness, but will have the light of life' (John 8:12).

When we turn our back on the teachings of Jesus, we live in spiritual darkness, being aware only of our own selfish desires. We think only in terms of what we haven't got, instead of counting our blessings. We think only in terms of what others can do for us, instead of concentrating on what we can do for others.

When we follow his teachings, we progress towards the light and forget about ourselves. We begin to understand that happiness lies, not in owning things, but in sharing things; not in striving to make ourselves happy, but in trying to make others happy. We achieve that state of inner peace which comes from knowing that, no matter how uncomfortable life may sometimes be, we wouldn't exchange the light for the shadow.

Listening

Sir Ranulph Fiennes, famous for his many expeditions, including the first polar circumnavigation of the earth, was asked what is the most important lesson life has taught him. He replied, 'To listen a lot more than talking. God gave us one tongue and two ears.' This is something worth remembering. If we listened twice as much as we talked, we would learn a lot more.

Jesus said that not everyone who claims to prophesy, drive out demons and perform many miracles in his name would enter the kingdom of heaven, but only those who do the will of his father who is in heaven (Matthew 7:21). Jesus was making the point that we can sometimes appear to be doing the will of God, when we are actually doing what we want and not what God wants, because we are not consulting God or listening to him.

Instead of getting caught up with doing what we want to do for God, or what we consider he would want us to do, we should make time, each day, to sincerely ask God to help us do his will, then patiently wait and listen for a response to our prayer.

Living Life to the Full

We sometimes hear that someone is 'living life to the full'. What do we mean by this? Do we mean that this person packs activity into every minute of the day; that they have lots of hobbies or interests; that they appear to be leading an exciting life?

Jesus said, 'I have come so that they may have life and have it to the full' (John 10:10). He came to teach us the way to live, and that way means putting others before ourselves. It doesn't mean being so busy with our own life that we don't have time for others. It doesn't mean asking, 'How can I get the most out of this day?', but rather, 'How can I put the most into this day?'; not, 'How can I make myself happy?', but rather, 'How can I make others happy?'; not 'What can I get out of life?', but rather, 'What can I put in to life?'.

Our life can be as action-packed and exciting as we want, but it's only by killing off our self-centredness that we become truly alive. It's only when our life is geared towards others, rather than ourselves, that we live life to the full.

Losing Your Life

A popular quiz question is: Which novel starts with the words, 'It was the best of times, it was the worst of times'? The answer is A Tale of Two Cities. The final words of the novel are probably just as well known: 'It is a far, far better thing that I do, than I have ever done; it is a far, far better rest that I go to than I have ever known.' These words are spoken by Sydney Carton, a scruffy drunkard, who describes himself as a good-for-nothing who has never done any good and never will. But at the end of the novel he gives up his life for another.

Jesus said: 'Whoever wants to save his life will lose it, but whoever loses his life for me will save it' (Luke 9:24; Matthew 16:25; Mark 8:35).

We don't have to literally lose our life, as Sydney Carton did, but we do have to strive for that love that seeks not for itself, but gives of itself. People who selfishly pursue their own desires lose their life in a futile search for happiness. But people who lose themselves in selflessness, by following the teachings of Christ, find true happiness.

Love

There's a song entitled: 'It Ain't What You Do, It's the Way That You Do It'. In 1 Corinthians 13, Paul says it ain't what you do, it's why you do it that's important.

He says anything – no matter how great – that's done without love is meaningless. He describes love as being patient and kind. He says love does not envy, nor does it boast and it is not proud. Love, according to Paul, is not rude, nor self-seeking, nor is it easily angered and it keeps no record of wrongs. He says love always protects, always trusts, always hopes, always perseveres. Love, he says, does not delight in evil, but rejoices with the truth.

Keeping to Paul's definition of love is rather a tall order, but if we can try to remember some of these points and occasionally examine the motives for our actions, it will help us to stop straying too far away from what we should be striving towards.

No matter how good our actions may appear to be, only by examining our conscience can we be sure that we are acting out of love.

Love One Another

K.I.S.S. This stands for 'Keep It Simple, Speaker' – a slogan used in training courses on effective communication: if you want to get a message across, keep it simple.

Jesus certainly kept his message simple – 'Love one another' (John 13:34). In his last hours with his disciples he told them that this was his only command. This short, simple command was so important that he repeated it again and again (John 15:12,17) before undergoing terrible suffering and death for love of us.

However, we find it so difficult to follow this command. Jesus didn't ask anything of us but this; yet we find it easier to do anything but this. He doesn't ask us to like everyone – that's impossible – but he does ask us to love everyone. There are lots of examples in the Bible of what is meant by 'love', the parable of the Good Samaritan being one.

We don't have to complicate our lives with lots of rules – just K.I.S.S. and love one another.

Love Your Enemies

Jesus said: 'Love your enemies. If you love those who love you, what credit is that to you? Even 'sinners' love those who love them. And if you do good to those who are good to you, what credit is that to you? Even 'sinners' do that.' (Luke 6:27; Matthew 5:44)

Most of us find this teaching extremely hard, if not impossible, to put into practice. Jesus is asking us to be kind to those who are not kind to us, to be considerate towards those who are not considerate towards us. We do sometimes manage to forgive someone who has been unkind to us. But no matter how forgiving, or understanding, we are, it is sometimes very difficult to feel kindly towards certain people, no matter how hard we try. In that situation we have to ask God to help us, because we are only human and we don't have the strength that is needed.

We might think Jesus is asking the impossible of us when he asks us to love our enemies. We can only achieve the impossible with the help of God.

Making Choices

In this world of uncertainties we are all looking for guarantees of the best way for living our life – for making the right choice in every decision. Experts and professionals can offer guidelines, but they can't give guarantees because every situation is different; a way of living that works for one person does not necessarily work for another. Likewise, because no two people are the same, what is the best way of living for one person is not always the best way for another.

Jesus said, 'I am the way' (John 14:6). Only God knows the best way of living for each and every one of his unique children. If we are prepared to put ourselves in the hands of a competent doctor when we are ill, how much more should we be prepared to put ourselves in the hands of our loving, all-knowing father, who wants only what is best for us. So, only by having complete trust in God at all times and in all situations can we guarantee that we are living in a way that is best for us.

Making Demands on God

Judith is one of the seven extra books in the Catholic Old Testament. It tells of an Israelite town besieged by the Assyrian army who cut off the town's water supply. The town chieftain promises to surrender if God does not rescue them within five days.

Judith is a beautiful, rich, young widow, who is also very devout. She tells the leaders of the people that they are wrong to test God with a promise of surrender if God does not rescue them in a set time. Instead, she puts her faith in God and sets out to save her people. This she does (in Old Testament gruesome style) by decapitating the army's captain. (There's a Donatello sculpture in Florence depicting this.) It's a rattling good tale that would be suitable for a Hollywood blockbuster.

However, the message for us is that we should not make demands on God. We should not adopt a 'I want you to do this for me, or else…' attitude. We should simply thank God for what we have received and trust that God will provide for us whenever, and in whatever way, is appropriate – which is usually the way we least expect.

Money

The saying 'Money is the root of all evil' can be very true. Money can split families and end friendships. It can literally cause murder. That is because we are brainwashed into believing that money brings happiness. And while we are busily pursuing that path to happiness, we are neglecting the true path to happiness.

Jesus was asked if it was right to pay taxes to Caesar. He pointed out that the denarius (the common Roman coin of that day) was issued by Caesar, with Caesar's portrait and inscription on, and was used for paying tax to him. Therefore, Jesus said: 'Give to Caesar what is Caesar's and to God what is God's' (Matthew 22:21).

Money is needed to pay our way in this world, but we should remember that that's all it does. Money provides physical comfort, but not spiritual comfort. Money is not our God and should not to be pursued at the cost of everything else. It is God that should be sought at the cost of everything else. The things that money cannot buy – selfless love, kindness, compassion – are the things that warm our hearts and these things can only be found with the help of God.

Neighbourliness

Concerning the command to love your neighbour as yourself, Jesus was asked: 'Who is my neighbour?' In reply he told the Parable of the Good Samaritan (Luke 10:25). There was a long history of hatred between Jews and Samaritans. The Samaritans had intermarried with foreigners so were regarded as not fully Jewish and had built their own temple in Samaria in opposition to the one in Jerusalem. In this parable the two people who ignore the injured man are both religious: a priest and a Levite, a high official in the temple and one slightly lower in status. It is the despised Samaritan who turns out to be the hero. This parable demonstrates that it is not status, colour, creed or gender that makes a person good. A good person is someone who treats every single person with compassion.

We may look down on people, thinking they are not as good as us when, in fact, they may be a lot kinder than we are. We erect barriers between ourselves and those who are different from us, but we should, as the Good Samaritan did, treat everyone as our neighbour.

Not Ours to Keep

We often hear parents tell their children: 'Play nicely. Share your toys.' Good parents want their children to be kind to other children, to learn to share and not to be mean-spirited. Likewise, our heavenly father wants his children to be kind to each other and to share what they have. We sometimes forget that everything we have has been given to us by our heavenly father and, therefore, is not ours to keep.

When Pilate told Jesus that he had the power either to free Jesus or to crucify him, Jesus answered, 'You would have no power over me if it were not given to you from above' (John 19:11).

Fearful people tend to cling to things for fear of losing them. They cling to power instead of sharing it; they cling to knowledge instead of sharing it; they cling to friends instead of sharing them. They don't realise that there's more than enough of everything for everybody. Shared power increases; shared knowledge increases, and shared friendships blossom and grow. The more you give away the more comes back to you, but what you cling to ends up rotting in your hands.

Patience

Patience is a virtue. The wisdom of these words was brought home to me by something that happened many years ago. One day, while I was washing the dishes, my three-year-old son came running into the kitchen, asking for a biscuit. 'Yes,' I said, 'but wait while I dry my hands so I can get the biscuit tin.' Without waiting, he reached up on tip-toe for the tin, knocked it off the shelf and it hit him on the head. He ended up in tears.

While I soothed him, saying, 'If only you'd waited, you wouldn't have hurt yourself,' I realised that we act like that with God. We get impatient for things to happen and, instead of trusting that the God who loves us will do what is right when the time is right, we take matters into our own hands, then wonder why it often ends in pain, not only to ourselves, but sometimes to others.

Peacemakers

Jesus said: 'Blessed are the peacemakers' (Matthew 5:9). We don't have to end wars to be peacemakers; there are many ways in which we can be peacemakers in our ordinary day-to-day lives.

For example, the tabloid press can sometimes whip up prejudice against all sorts of people, and we can easily get caught up in it. We can be peacemakers by not going along with this, but by trying to put ourselves in the shoes of any persecuted persons.

Also, instead of joining in with friends or colleagues when they complain about other people, we can try to put forward possible reasons for the other person's behaviour, or suggest that things are not always as they seem – try to help them see the other side of the coin.

Peace will only come when we are prepared to forget our pride, give up on any disagreements we have with others, and make our peace with whoever we are in disagreement with. When we are prepared to do this, we can join the band of blessed peacemakers.

Perseverance

'If at first you don't succeed, try, try, try again', says the proverb.

When Jesus explained the Parable of the Sower he said that the seed that fell into the good soil and produced its crop a hundredfold represents people who have persevered (Luke 8:15).

Perseverance is mentioned a number of times in the Bible. Peter mentions it (2 Peter 1:6) and James speaks of trials and temptations producing perseverance, saying 'blessed is anyone who perseveres' (1:12). Paul mentions perseverance in most of his letters: in Romans 5:3; in 2 Corinthians 12:12, and in 2 Thessalonians 1:4 and 3:5. he tells Timothy to persevere (1 Timothy 4:16), and tells the Hebrews 'You will need to persevere' (Hebrews 10:36), and urges 'with perseverance keep running in the race' (12:1). These writers knew how tempting it is to give up when the going gets tough.

In our spiritual life most things are very difficult – keeping faith, practising patience, practising tolerance, or learning to forgive – and no matter how hard we try we fail from time to time. But failing is quite different from not even trying. All we can do is try, try, try again.

Poor in Spirit

Jesus said: 'Blessed are the poor in spirit, for the Kingdom of Heaven is theirs.' (Matthew 5:3). What did he mean?

If we are poor and without the means of providing for ourselves, we depend on others to help us – the way children do. Therefore, if we are poor in spirit, we depend on God to help us. We are poor in spirit when we realise our own helplessness and put our whole trust in God. To be poor in spirit means to be humble, not self-righteous, before God. We are poor in spirit when we do not have security from our own resources, but when our feelings of security lie in God. We are poor in spirit when we are grateful to God for whatever we have and not smugly self-satisfied with our achievements.

The opposite of being poor in spirit is when we trust in things that are not God. Having possessions is not wrong (Abraham was a rich man), but our attitude towards our possessions can be wrong. Our possessions should not possess us. We are poor in spirit when we know that it is the love of God, not possessions, that makes us rich.

Prayer

Ann Widdecombe, when asked if God has ever spoken to her, replied, 'God speaks to us all in different ways – it's up to us whether we hear him'. The problem is that most of us like to talk more than we like to listen.

When Jesus taught his followers how to pray (Matthew 6:5) he told them not to make a big show of it, but to do it in private, and not to babble like pagans who think they will be heard because of their many words. He then went on to give them a very simple prayer that we know as the Lord's Prayer. He told them to look upon God as their heavenly father; to try to do God's will; to ask God to provide their needs for each day; to forgive anyone who sinned against them and to ask their heavenly father to forgive their sins, and to help them resist temptation.

If we can remember to keep our prayers simple by asking God to help us in everything we do, trusting that God will help us, waiting patiently for that help, trying to do whatever feels right, then God will be communicating with us.

Preaching

Edgar Guest (1881-1959), the popular American poet, wrote a poem, the first twelve lines of which are:

I'd rather see a sermon than hear one any day;
I'd rather one walk with me than merely show the way.
The eye's a better pupil and more willing than the ear,
Fine counsel is confusing, but example's always clear;
And the best of all the preachers are the men who live their creeds,
For to see good put into action is what everybody needs.
I soon can learn to do it if you'll let me see it done;
I can watch your hands in action, but your tongue too fast may run
And the lecture you deliver may be very wise and true,
But I'd rather get my lessons by observing what you do;
For I might misunderstand you and the high advice you give,
But there's no misunderstanding how you act and how you live.

St Francis of Assisi is said to have told his brethren: 'Preach the Gospel and sometimes use words'.

Wise words worth remembering.

Prejudice

How often do we hear expressions like, 'That's typical of a southerner'. Some northerners are prejudiced against southerners; some southerners are prejudiced against northerners. Some rich people are prejudiced against poor people; some poor people are prejudiced against rich people. Some white people are prejudiced against black people; some black people are prejudiced against white people. Some Catholics are prejudiced against Protestants; some Protestants are prejudiced against Catholics. The list is endless. Most of us have at least one prejudice; it seems to be part of our human condition.

When Jesus commanded his disciples to love one another, he said: 'By this all men will know that you are my disciples, if you love one another' (John 13:35). He isn't asking us to love only members of our own little group, but ALL disciples, whether rich, poor, black, white, southerner, northerner, Catholic or Protestant.

One of the most difficult things we have to strive against is being biased. We may be truly ecumenical, or genuinely not racist, but hold stereotypical views about lower/upper class people, or about those who live in the north/south. We need to constantly fight against our prejudices.

Pride

Pride comes before a fall. This certainly was true in the story of Adam and Eve in Genesis 2. God gave them everything they needed for a happy life, telling them that they could eat from any tree in the garden of Eden, but not from the tree of the knowledge of good and evil. They were easily persuaded to forget God's goodness towards them, and to believe that eating from this tree would make them as great as God, therefore having no further need of him. It was this act of pride that caused their downfall.

Like Adam and Eve, we are tempted to take for granted everything that God has given us. If we don't count our blessings, we can become dissatisfied with what we have and feel we deserve more.

Once we stop being grateful to God for what we have and start believing that we are worthy of better things, we are guilty of the sin of pride – heading for a fall.

Priorities

Try this: fill a large jar with golf balls; then pour in pebbles, giving a light shake, so they roll into the spaces between the golf balls; finish off by pouring sand in until the jar is completely full. Now empty the jar and reverse the process: sand, then pebbles, then golf balls. You'll find there's not enough room for all the golf balls.

If we think of the golf balls as being God, the most important thing in our life; the pebbles as our fellow humans, second in importance; and the sand as the other things in our life, it's easy to see that if we give priority to the least important things in our life, we don't have enough space left for God.

When Martha complains to Jesus that Mary is listening to him instead of helping her, he tells Martha that she worries about many things, yet few are needed. 'Mary has chosen the better part' (Luke 10:38). He is telling her to put the important things first, then all the other things will fall into place.

So, if we don't have time for short daily prayer, we should remind ourselves of Mary, Martha and the golf balls.

Problems

Do you ever feel weighed down with worries, or overwhelmed with problems? We all feel like that from time to time. It's at times like this that it helps to remember the words of Jesus: 'Come to me, all you who are weary and burdened, and I will give you rest' (Matthew 11:28).

If a child asked a loving parent for help, would that parent refuse? If we, the children of God, ask for help, will God refuse? We need to trust that God will help us. We need to hand over our worries or problems with the same wholeheartedness that we would hand over heavy bags of shopping to a trusted friend who's offered a helping hand. We then need to stop worrying, knowing that the problem is now out of our hands. If we do this, solutions will come to us.

Once we realise that we are not great enough to solve every problem and, like children, we need God's help, we can put ourselves in God's hands, stop worrying, and our problems will gradually resolve themselves in ways we least expect.

Rejection

Christians believe Isaiah 53 to be a prophesy of the coming of Jesus Christ. It says: 'He was despised and rejected by men, a man of sorrows, and familiar with suffering… He took up our infirmities and carried our sorrows… He was pierced for our transgressions, crushed for our iniquities… by his wounds we are healed… He was oppressed and afflicted, yet he did not open his mouth; he was led like a lamb to the slaughter… he had done no violence, nor was any deceit in his mouth… He bore the sin of many.' The word 'despised' is repeated, followed by 'and we esteemed him not'.

How many of us could bear to be despised and rejected when we'd done nothing wrong. We all want to be esteemed. We all want to be popular and have people admire us. However, sometimes we have to be prepared to be unpopular in order to make a stand for what is right. We have to decide whether we want to do what God wants, or what certain people want. If we ever have to make this choice, we can think about Isaiah 53.

Retribution

In our current culture of suing at the first opportunity, we would do well to remember what Jesus taught. He taught the opposite to what was accepted as normal. He was speaking of financial retribution when he said we should not claim 'an eye for an eye', and that 'If someone wants to sue you and take your tunic, let him have your cloak as well' (Matthew 5:40). A cloak was more valuable than a tunic. He was advising against getting involved in lawsuits, but to sort out differences with a kind and generous spirit.

We can insist on our 'rights', on 'getting our pound of flesh', simply to prove that we are in the right and the other person is in the wrong – but at what cost? The price can be untold misery.

On the other hand, we can approach the situation with a generous heart, willing to come to an agreement that is most beneficial to all concerned and trying to give a little more than we take. This sort of attitude makes friends instead of enemies and makes the world a happier place.

Road to Life

'Keep on the straight and narrow' is an expression we use to remind ourselves to lead a good life.

Jesus said: Enter through the narrow gate. For wide is the gate and broad is the road that leads to destruction, and many enter through it. But small is the gate and narrow the road that leads to life, and only a few find it (Matthew 7:13).

Physically, it's easier to walk on a wide path that gives us the freedom to roam where we please than it is to walk on a narrow path where we're restricted. Likewise, it's easier to please ourselves and do the wrong thing than to restrict ourselves to doing the right thing. It's easier to ignore someone in need than get involved in helping. It's easier to make excuses for not helping others than it is to put ourselves out for them.

Spiritually, we are all travelling on a path through life. If we always choose the easy way we are on the broad road. If we constantly question our motives and chose what we believe to be morally right, we will stick to the narrow path.

Seek and You Will Find

You can take a horse to water, but you can't make it drink. How true that is. We all know how impossible it is to help someone who doesn't want to be helped. Doctors can help us only if we're prepared to take the medicine, however unpleasant it might be, or follow the medical advice, no matter how unwelcome it might be.

Likewise, God can't help us to live better lives if we're not prepared to ask for help, listen for an answer and act on it, no matter how unwelcome it might be – such as, swallow your pride, or forgive someone who has hurt you.

Jesus said: 'Ask and it will be given to you; seek and you will find; knock and the door will be opened to you. For everyone who asks receives; he who seeks finds; and to him who knocks, the door will be opened.' (Matthew 7:7)

These words show clearly that everyone, without exception, will receive help if it is asked for. But we can't expect others to do it for us; we need to make the request ourselves and it has to be a sincere wish to find a better way.

Seek First The Kingdom of God

If we conducted a survey, asking people what would make them happy, we would get a variety of answers, such as: money, travel, successful career, loving partner, nice home, and so on. Not many people would answer: 'Finding the kingdom of God.'

Jesus said: 'Seek first the kingdom of God, and all these things will be given to you as well.' (Matthew 6:33; Luke 12:31).

The message here is that we should put God first and everything else will follow on. A nice home, a loving partner, money, etc., will give us a certain amount of happiness, but without a right relationship with God these things will not give us true inner contentment and security. When we get our priorities the wrong way around, we forget about God in our relentless pursuit of the things we think will make us happy, only to find that once we've attained them they don't bring us the deep and lasting happiness we thought they would.

On the other hand, when we make our first priority that of doing God's will and caring about our fellow humans, other things come along without undue effort on our part and we find true happiness.

Selflessness

'What's in it for me?' 'Look after number one!' We sometimes hear this, don't we? The opposite attitude to this is found in the Book of Ruth. This tells the story of a widow, Naomi, whose two sons die, leaving her with two daughters-in-law, Ruth and Orpah. Naomi feels her life is empty – she has lost her husband and now her two sons, and she has no grandchildren. She decides to return to her homeland.

Naomi tells her daughters-in-law to go back to their families, where they will have a chance of finding another husband and a better life. Orpah departs, but Ruth's refusal to leave Naomi highlights her loyalty and selfless devotion to her desolate mother-in-law. Ruth's commitment to Naomi is complete, even though it holds no prospect for her.

In order to look after Naomi, Ruth goes to a land where she is a foreigner from a despised people. Ruth, a vulnerable young woman, nevertheless undertakes to provide for her mother-in-law and in doing so finds a kind and rich husband and bears a son, giving new life to Naomi. Ruth was to become great-grandmother to David, ultimately an ancestor of Christ.

Sharing

The Feeding of the Five Thousand (Matthew 14:13; Mark 6:32; Luke 9:10; John 6:1) is a familiar story. Jesus tells his disciples to share all that they have – five loaves and two fish – with a crowd of five thousand. There is plenty for everyone.

This story shows that when we share what we have, it does not decrease, but increases. Things that are jealously guarded – be they possessions, affection, time, or power – and never shared with others, shrivel up and stagnate.

When we welcome people into our home, we are sharing our home with them; when we bestow genuine affection on others, we are sharing our affection; when we give of our time, we are sharing it with others, and when we invite others to join us in decision-making, we are sharing our power with others. All these things increase, and do not decrease, our happiness.

A good parent gives its child all of its love and if a second child arrives that parent does not reduce its love by half, but rather gives the second child the same amount of its love too, and the same for a third and fourth child. The more love is shared the more it grows.

Sincerity

In The Sermon on the Mount, Jesus said: 'Blessed are the pure of heart, for they shall see God' (Matthew 5:8). What does it mean to be pure of heart? It means to be sincere. It means not being hypocritical, not having hidden intentions, not wearing different masks. It means not compromising our beliefs, no matter what the difficulties.

We can be tempted to take the easy way out of an awkward situation by being insincere, hypocritical, or compromising our beliefs, then make excuses for our behaviour. But if we put ourselves in God's hands we are given the strength and wisdom to be sincere in everything we do. We can fool ourselves, or convince ourselves, that what we are doing is right. But if we want to be pure of heart we have to ask God to help us be sincere and help us to do the right thing for the right reasons.

If we want to be pure of heart we have to open our heart to God. Just as closed eyes cannot see, neither can closed hearts, so only those who open their hearts to God will perceive God.

Spirit of Life

A weekend newspaper supplement recently published extracts from a book by a writer who tried to live the ultimate biblical life. He prepared by spending five hours a day for four weeks reading the whole Bible from Genesis to Revelation, searching for every rule and suggestion, resulting in 72 pages of guidelines for everyday living. He then spent a year avoiding: certain foods; certain clothes; cutting his hair; contact with women (including his wife) at certain times, and working on the Sabbath. He also tried not to lie, covet, or be lustful. At the end of the year he says he is still agnostic.

Jesus did not live by the letter of the law. Luke 13:10 and Matthew 12:1 tell of Jesus healing on the Sabbath, much to the outrage of the synagogue rulers and Pharisees, who then plotted how they might kill Jesus.

In 2 Corinthians 3:1 Paul speaks of 'a new covenant, written not with ink but with the Spirit of the living God, not on tablets of stone but on tablets of human hearts – for the letter kills, but the Spirit gives life.'

If we read the Bible, let us search for the spirit of love.

Spiritual Maturity

The novelist, George Eliot, believed that we have to work hard to shed our spiritual childishness in order to reach spiritual maturity; that we have to give up our childish self-centredness and learn to be selfless. In her novel, Middlemarch, the young idealistic heroine, Dorothea, who yearns to pursue some large, noble cause and believes her marriage will help her achieve this aim, quickly discovers that this is not to be: so begins her painful journey to spiritual maturity.

St. Paul said: When I was a child, I talked like a child, I thought like a child, I reasoned like a child. When I became a man, I put childish ways behind me (1 Corinthians 13:11).

Just as the well-meaning, but somewhat egotistic, Dorothea eventually learns that life does not go according to her plans, we too have to learn this lesson. We cannot stamp our foot, like a spoilt child, when things don't go our way. We have to learn that God has a plan for each and every one of us and we have to willingly, patiently and lovingly pray that Thy will, not my will, be done.

Suffering

Sometimes we feel we are being made to suffer for something that is not of our doing, and life can seem very unfair. When this happens we tend to ask: 'What have I done to deserve this?' 'Why has this happened to me?'

When things go wrong we can be tempted to blame God: 'Why did God let this happen?' 'How can a loving God allow this to happen?' But this attitude simply makes us bitter and more unhappy.

Instead, we can draw some comfort from the thought that we are not alone in our suffering. We can remind ourselves that Jesus suffered a cruel death when he had done nothing wrong.

If we feel that we are being made to suffer unfairly, we should not turn against God, but turn to God for the strength to cope. We need to remind ourselves that when we hurt, God, as our loving father, hurts with us.

Superiority

'He's been here so long, he thinks he owns the place!' How often have we heard that? Unfortunately, this attitude can be found in all walks of life – in the workplace, in social clubs, in voluntary organisations and in churches. Those who have been there the longest think they are in some way superior to newcomers.

In the Parable of the Workers in the Vineyard (Matthew 20:1), worldly ways are turned upside down when the master treats the newcomers the same as those that have been there longest and, in fact, says that the first shall be last and the last shall be first.

The problem with belonged to something for a long time is that it can create a sense of having earned a position of superiority, thus creating inequality and an absence of humility. Regardless of how long we have been a part of any group, we should ask ourselves if we arrogantly believe that we are of more value than others, or if we humbly acknowledge that others have as much to offer as we do.

Talents

The Parable of the Talents (Matthew 25:14; Luke 19:12) tells of a master who gave his three servants some talents (coins). The first two put their talents to good use, doubling their worth, and so shared in their master's happiness. The third servant, ungratefully accusing his master of hardness and dishonesty, buried his talent, putting it to no use at all. Our use of the word 'talent', meaning a gift or ability, is derived from this parable.

We have each been given different abilities, but there are some abilities that every single person has. If we care about others we have the opportunity to use these abilities every time we come into contact with another person. We can use our ability to lift someone's spirits with a smile or a kind word. We can use our ability to lighten someone's load by simply listening when they need to talk. Kindness has a knock-on effect, so if we use our God-given abilities for the benefit of others, they multiply, and we share in the happiness they bring. If we choose to bury them deep within ourselves, we bring happiness to nobody, including ourselves.

Temptation

Temptation is around us all the time. We are constantly tempted to do things to make ourselves feel better. We can be tempted to eat more than is good for us, or consume more alcohol than is good for us. We can be tempted by worldly goods, spending more than we can afford on 'retail therapy'. We can be tempted by egotism to show how great we are. Giving in to these temptations may make us feel good in the short term, but the long term consequences of our actions can lead to much unhappiness. Things that we do to make ourselves feel better, knowing that they're not good for us, have little lasting positive effect.

In Luke 4:1 (Matthew 4:1; Mark 1:12) we're told that Jesus was tempted in the desert. He was tempted by food, after fasting for forty days; he was tempted with worldly possessions, and he was tempted to show his greatness. He fought against all these temptations by keeping focussed on God's will.

Like Jesus, we can only resist the temptation for self-satisfaction by turning to God for help, and it is only by striving for self-forgetfulness that we find ourselves feeling much better.

The Good Shepherd

In John Chapter 10, Jesus refers to himself as the good shepherd who lays down his life for the sheep because they belong to him, unlike the hired hand who, when he sees the wolf coming, abandons the sheep. He says the sheep know his voice, so follow when he calls, but will never follow a stranger.

A good parent would lay down their life for their child. They would not abandon their child when trouble comes along. Their care of their child is a labour of love; they're not paid a wage for what they do. A hired hand may not feel the same way.

Just as a child recognises the voice of the one who truly loves them, so we too must learn to recognise the voice of the one who truly loves us. We must not follow the voices of those who don't care about us. These voices tempt us with empty promises of happiness and a false sense of security. Only the one who truly loves us – as only a loving parent can – is able to promise us true happiness and true peace of mind.

Tolerance

We've all thought, at some time, 'I'd never do that,' when we witness someone acting in, what we consider to be, an unacceptable way. It is only if we find ourselves doing the very things we have frowned on that we learn to be more tolerant of other people's weaknesses.

At the Last Supper, Jesus predicted that all his disciples would fall away. Peter said, 'Even if all fall away, I will not' (Matthew 26:31; Mark 14:27). Peter thought it possible for any of the others to do this, but not himself. When Peter realised that he had disowned Jesus, he 'wept bitterly' (Matthew 26:75; Mark 14:72). Peter must have felt great shame when he found himself guilty of the one weakness he didn't believe he possessed. This experience will have taught him humility and greater tolerance of other people's weaknesses.

Jesus will have realised that Peter's humbling experience made Peter a better person. Jesus forgave him and, in fact, commissioned him to care for his sheep (John 21:16).

When we find ourselves guilty of weaknesses for which we have condemned others, we need to remember that God forgives anyone who truly repents, and we need to learn humility and tolerance from the experience.

Trust in God

The miracle of the feeding of the five thousand (Matthew 14:13; Mark 6:32; Luke 9:10; John 6:1) tells us that crowds of people left the towns and followed Jesus on foot to a lonely place. When evening came, the disciples were all for sending the people away to trek to the nearest villages to buy themselves some food, but Jesus refused to turn them away hungry and he provided them with as much food as they wanted.

Those people left the safety of the towns, where food and shelter were guaranteed, in search of the one they believed could help them. If we want God to help us, we have to believe – as those people did. We need to leave behind our old ways that are familiar and therefore feel safe, and move forward, with faith, into new ways of thinking and acting, with no guarantee of how things will turn out.

When evening came and hunger set in, those people may have begun to regret having ventured on that journey. When we embark on our spiritual journey, we too, at times, may suffer some discomfort and begin to regret having started, but when we trust in God we will never be turned away spiritually hungry.

Unity

The word 'shibboleth' is a word used as a test for detecting people from another district or country by their pronunciation. It is, therefore, a way of separating one people from another. It comes from chapter 12 of the Book of Judges which describes how the Gileadites captured the fords of the Jordan and anyone wanting to cross was asked to say the word 'shibboleth'. The dialect of their enemies, the Ephraimites, did not include a 'sh' sound, so those who pronounced it 'sibboleth' were killed. It says that 42,000 Ephraimites were killed at that time.

There are a lot of stories in the Old Testament that describe conflict and division, but in the New Testament Jesus is constantly teaching us to love one another, to 'all be one', to be 'perfected in unity' (John Chapter 17). A theme in Luke is Jesus breaking down barriers between people: with Samaritans; with tax-collectors; with sinners – 'more joy in heaven over one repentant sinner' (15:7), and treating women as equal to men. Every time we are tempted with 'shibboleth', let us remember the teaching of Jesus.

Wisdom

In the novels of Charles Dickens, children are often portrayed as saintly and adults as sinners. This is because Dickens believed that children, untainted by the world, are closer to God than adults who can become corrupted by worldly vices, such as greed, pride, or dishonesty. In the novel Great Expectations, however, it is young Pip who falls under the influence of the sophisticated Estella and pursues an education to become a gentleman, consequently becoming ashamed of his foster-father, Joe, 'a mere blacksmith'. In the end Pip realises the emptiness of worldly values. It is Joe, the man without education, who, throughout the story, retains the true values.

Jesus said: You, Father, have hidden these things from the wise and learned, and revealed them to little children (Matthew 11:25; Luke 10:21).

We don't have to be literally 'children' in order to have God's ways revealed to us, and there is nothing wrong with being wise and learned. But we do have to come before God as 'children', humbly acknowledging our ignorance compared with his wisdom.

Arrogance is not a part of Joe, the blacksmith, who, with his gentle heart, is a true gentleman. That's why the wisdom of God is revealed to him.

Worry

An American pathologist, Lewis Thomas, said: 'Worrying is the most natural and spontaneous of all human functions. It is time to acknowledge this, perhaps even to learn to do it better.'

Certainly, worrying is something we all do, to a greater or lesser extent.

Jesus urges us not to worry: 'Look at the birds of the air; they do not sow or reap or store away in barns, and yet your heavenly father feeds them. Are you not much more valuable than they? Who of you by worrying can add a single hour to his life?' (Matthew 6:26; Luke 12:22).

The reason we worry is because we take everything on our own shoulders instead of trusting in God. We keep forgetting that we do not have to do it all. We keep forgetting that our heavenly father loves us more than we can begin to imagine. If we have complete trust in God and concentrate on the matters of today, tomorrow will look after itself.

Instead of acknowledging and learning to worry better, as Lewis Thomas advises, we should acknowledge God's love for us and learn better to trust in him, as Jesus advises.

Worthiness

'Why should I help them? They're not worth it!' How often do we think that? That's what Jonah thought when God asked him to help some people. Instead of going to help them Jonah promptly jumped on a ship heading in the opposite direction and, we are told, ended up inside a fish for three days.

He relented and did help, but still felt they didn't deserve it. God had to come to Jonah again and explain to him that he had no right to decide who is, or who is not, worthy of help.

Something worth remembering next time we think 'Why should I?'

Wrongdoing

When Peter asked Jesus if he should forgive his brother up to seven times, Jesus answered, 'Not seven times, but seventy-seven times.' (Matthew 18:21). Jesus also said, 'If your brother sins, rebuke him, and if he repents, forgive him' (Luke 17:3). So, although Jesus taught forgiveness, he wasn't encouraging us to forgive wrongdoing without trying to do something about it.

Forgiveness doesn't involve excusing a wrongdoing, nor ignoring or denying it, nor turning a blind eye, or pretending it didn't happen. Such responses indulge wrongdoing, rather than dealing with it. Sometimes we don't realise that we're acting wrongly, or we're reluctant to examine our actions and motives, so if nobody points out our faults, we carry on.

We should confront a wrongdoer humbly, not arrogantly and self-righteously, and we should do it privately, not publicly, 'If your brother sins against you, go and show him his fault, just between the two of you' (Matthew 18:15)

We are not meant to seek revenge or bear a grudge, nor are we meant to confront people in order to get something off our chest and make ourselves feel better, but to sincerely help the other person see what they've done wrong.

Christmas
The Light of the World

The Light of the World, a famous painting by the Pre-Raphaelite artist, William Holman Hunt, hangs in St Paul's Cathedral. It is based on Christ's description of himself and his mission: 'I am the light of the world: he that followeth me shall not walk in darkness, but shall have the light of life' (John 8:12); also Revelation 3:20 'Here I am! I stand at the door and knock'.

The scene is set at night and is of Christ holding a lantern and knocking at a door. The night-time setting symbolises the darkness into which Christ is the bearer of light. There are weeds growing outside the door, which symbolise the neglect of spiritual values; the closed door symbolises the obstinately shut mind; and the door has no outside handle, because it is the door of the human heart that can only be opened from the inside.

As we approach Christmas, this painting can serve as a reminder. The current 'weeds' of the world are the over-the-top commercialisation of Christmas, which cause us to forget the true meaning of Christmas – a celebration of the birth of Christ who came as the light of the world.

Christmas

A Christmas Carol

The story 'A Christmas Carol' is so well known that a mean person has become known as a Scrooge. The Ghost of Christmas Past shows that Scrooge was not always mean, but that he allowed money to become his 'Idol', his 'master-passion'. Young Scrooge's loving fiancée, Belle, releases him from their engagement because he has altered; he now weighs everything by gain and sees love as of little worth or value. His hope for the future now lies in money, not love. Scrooge is an example of how easy it is to slip into holding the wrong values.

Christmas is a celebration of the birth of Jesus who came to teach us that love of our fellow beings is the most important and valuable thing. We don't need money in order to be generous. We can be generous with our time by patiently listening to others; we can be generous with our abilities by offering to help others.

The story of A Christmas Carol shows that it is never too late to change our ways. Like Scrooge, in the final chapter, we need to embrace the true Christmas message of love and kindness towards our fellow beings.

Christmas

Shepherds and Magi

In Chapter Two of Luke's Gospel we are told that an angel appeared to some shepherds and told them that a Saviour had been born. Shepherds were poor and ignorant people, so were not well regarded. However, the birth of Jesus was not made known to leaders, but to these lowly inhabitants. This is a foretaste of the type of man this baby was to become. The Pharisees and Herodians knew that Jesus was no respecter of human rank when they said to him, 'We know that you are an honest man, that you are not afraid of anyone, because human rank means nothing to you' (Mark 12:14; Matthew 22:16; Luke 20:21).

In Chapter Two of Matthew's Gospel we are told that Magi from the east came looking for the one 'born king of the Jews'. This reference to the king of the Jews indicates that the Magi were Gentiles. The gifts they brought show that they were rich.

Jesus came as a Saviour for everyone – rich, poor, Jew, Gentile. All we need is to be poor in spirit and rich in humility to receive his message.

Post-Christmas

Many people will be glad to have Christmas over for another year, because for them it's a time of family squabbles.

In a poem by Wendy Cope entitled '30th December' she says: 'Christmas was a muddle of turkey bones and muted quarrelling'. She goes on to say: 'The visitors have left' and concludes: 'If only this could be Christmas now'. There will be a lot of people who can relate to these sentiments.

Jesus said: 'Who are my mother and my brothers? Whoever does God's will is my brother and sister and mother.' (Mark 3:33; Matthew 12:48; Luke 8:21) He was saying that membership of God's spiritual family is more important than membership of our human families.

Christmas is a time for family get-togethers and if we are fortunate enough to have family members who practise the selfless love taught by Jesus, we can enjoy their company at all times and particularly so at Christmas. However, if some of our family members selfishly do their own will rather than God's will, it can make Christmas a miserable time. In this case, we can only be thankful for what we have, and hope that others will eventually join God's spiritual family.

New Year

New Wineskins

On 1st January we might make New Year resolutions; perhaps resolve to replace old ways with new ways.

Jesus said: 'Men do not pour new wine into old wineskins. If they do, the skins will burst, the wine will run out and the wineskins will be ruined. No, they pour new wine into new wineskins, and both are preserved' (Matthew 9:17; Mark 2:22; Luke 5:37).

In ancient times goatskins were used to hold wine. As the fresh grape juice fermented, the wine would expand and the new wineskin would stretch. But a used skin, already stretched, would break. Jesus was saying that newness cannot be confined within old forms.

If we want to change our ways, we have to change completely if we want it to last. For example, it's no use putting on an appearance of kindness, while in our heart we are still unkind. Just like the old wineskins, our outward appearance won't last when what we are feeling inside ferments. We need to have a change of heart; replace our old feelings of unkindness with new feelings of kindness. Then the love that is shown on the outside will be the same as the love that is felt on the inside, so will last.

New Year

Resoluteness

How many New Year resolutions will quickly be broken? It's easy, isn't it, on New Year's Eve, to declare that we are going to do a certain thing. But when the going gets tough, we're not as resolute as we thought we were.

Jesus told Peter: 'Before the cock crows, you will have disowned me three times.' Peter replied, 'Even if I have to die with you, I will never disown you' (Matthew 26:34; Mark 14:30). But fear overcame Peter and he was not as resolute as he thought he was.

However, after the Holy Spirit came upon Peter at Pentecost (Acts 2), his bravery and resoluteness knew no bounds. He fearlessly went out and preached about Jesus. He was arrested and brought before the same rulers who had condemned Jesus. They were astonished at Peter's courage. When they commanded him not to preach about Jesus, he refused.

We can learn from Peter's experience that no matter how much we want to do something, we can't always manage it under our own steam. Maybe a good resolution would be to rely more on the Holy Spirit.

Epiphany

Gifts

On 6th January we celebrate the arrival of the three wise men bearing gifts for the baby Jesus.

Even though we don't always realise it, every single one of us is born with gifts – we are given gifts that money can't buy.

A small minority of people are born with an outstanding gift in such spheres as music, art, sport or athletics, while the majority of us may feel that we were born with no particular gift at all. However, just as those 'gifted' people have to practice every day in order to use their gift to the full, we too need to realise what our gift is and practice it every day in order to use it to the full.

We've all been given the gift of helping others in a variety of ways. We simply need to go out every day bearing our gifts and use them to the full for the benefit of others.

Epiphany

Spiritual Journey

On January 6th, Christians celebrate the Wise Men's arrival at Bethlehem. It is believed that they travelled over 1,000 miles. Their long journey would not have been an easy one. They left behind the comforts of home to travel through unknown territory. They did not know precisely where they were going, or exactly what they were going to find when they got there. They may have taken some wrong paths and had to double back. But despite all this, they carried on.

There is a message here for us. When we embark on our spiritual journey, it may seem difficult. We may feel that we're leaving behind everything that makes us feel safe and comfortable. We may not know what lies ahead of us and may feel confused. We may sometimes seem to be taking one step forward and two steps back. But despite all this – like the Wise Men – we must persevere.

Wise men – and wise women – know how important it is to find their spiritual saviour.

Valentine's Day

'Love' must be one of the most frequently used words in popular songs – at least, it was in my youth. We had 'All You Need is Love'; 'Can't Buy Me Love', and 'I Don't Want to Live in a World without Love', to name but a few. The word 'love' is also one of the most frequently used words in the Bible. The songwriters' definition of 'love' is assumed to be romantic love between two people, but the Bible definition is a truly selfless love that we should give even to our enemies.

Jesus said, 'Everyone will know that you are my disciples if you have love for one another' (John 13:35).

The atmosphere created by people who radiate this selfless love is one of a happiness that really is 'all you need' and is something that you 'can't buy'. On the other hand, in a cut-throat, dog-eat-dog sort of environment, with people who don't care about anyone but themselves, the atmosphere is miserable and no amount of money, or other distractions, can relieve it – it really is the sort of world that we 'don't want to live in'.

St David's Day

St David's Day is celebrated on 1st March. It is claimed that David lived for over 100 years and died on Tuesday 1 March 589. He was a teacher and preacher, and founded monasteries and churches in Wales. The Monastic Rule of David prescribed that monks had to pull the plough themselves without the help of animals; to drink only water; to eat only bread with salt and herbs; and to spend the evenings in prayer, reading and writing. No personal possessions were allowed: to say 'my book' was an offence. Rather a harsh way of life, we may think.

However, in a world where people are acquiring more and more personal possessions, and placing more importance on these possessions than on their relationship with God and neighbour, St David's Day reminds us that there are some things more important than personal possessions.

St Patrick's Day

It is believed that when St Patrick was about sixteen, he was captured and carried off as a slave to Ireland. After six years he escaped and eventually became a priest. He returned to Ireland as a missionary in 433.

He is most known for driving the snakes from Ireland. There are no snakes in Ireland and probably never have been. In many old pagan religions, serpent symbols were common and often worshipped, so Patrick's driving the snakes from Ireland was probably symbolic of putting an end to the worshipping of false idols.

Just as St Patrick rid Ireland of the worshipping of false idols, so we need to rid ourselves of the worshipping of false idols. Our false idols consist of money, status, possessions, power – anything we consider more important than God.

St George's Day

On 23rd April we remember St. George, the Patron Saint of England. Legend has it that George was a Christian who became a high-ranking officer in the Roman army. The story is that a dragon made its nest at the spring that provided water for the city of Cyrene, so each day, in order to collect water, the citizens had to lure the dragon away with a human sacrifice. George, passing through on his travels, slew the dragon, so the grateful citizens abandoned their paganism and converted to Christianity. When he criticized the Emperor's decision to persecute Christians, George was tortured by being lacerated on a wheel of swords then executed by decapitation on April 23, 303. The witness of his suffering convinced some pagans to become Christians.

Thankfully, we don't have to fight dragons, or suffer persecution, torture or execution. However, no matter how ordinary and uneventful our day-to-day living might be, our decisions and our actions affect other people, without us even realising it. Perhaps we should remind ourselves of what we believe in and let our decisions and actions reflect those beliefs.

Shrove Tuesday

According to tradition, Shrove Tuesday was the last day for using up butter, fat and eggs before giving them up for Lent – hence the pancakes. Nowadays people give up a variety of things for Lent and donate the money saved to charities working with less fortunate people for whom every day in the year is one of doing without the things we take for granted.

Giving up something every now and again is good for spiritual growth. Such things as gluttony, greed, lust, vanity, avarice, are permanent features of life and constant temptations. Giving up something for a while is an exercise in resisting temptation and helps to stop personal cravings dictating our actions.

Giving up something – setting aside our desires – now and again, helps slow down our reactions to our cravings. People who constantly contrive to get their own way and aim at pleasing themselves – having what they want when they want it – don't find inner peace.

Inner peace comes from concerning ourselves with other people's needs rather than our own and being aware that sometimes we have to set aside our desires for the good of others.

Lent

Change of Heart

Lent is associated with penance. Penance is associated with 'sackcloth and ashes'; with doing difficult or painful things – the dictionary definition is 'self-punishment as reparation for guilt'. But the word 'penance' is derived from the word 'repent', and the original meaning of the word 'repent' is 'a change of mind and heart'.

The first words of Jesus in Mark's Gospel are: 'The time has come. The kingdom of God is near. Repent and believe the good news' (1:15). So, Jesus was not asking us to inflict physical punishment on ourselves, but to have a change of heart, to have a change of attitude towards God and the way we treat others. To do this may cause us discomfort, or even pain, but it is needed if we truly want to repent.

For those of us who have not yet had a change of heart, Lent might be a good time to start thinking about what Jesus asks us to do. For those of us who have experienced a change of heart, Lent may be a good time to think more deeply about what is asked of us.

Lent

Forty Days

Lent is a forty-day period. (Sundays celebrate the resurrection of Jesus, so are not counted as part of Lent.) There are many references to forty days in the Bible: it rained for forty days and forty nights during Noah's flood, and Moses spent forty days and forty nights on Mount Sinai with God. The Gospels say that after his baptism at the Jordan, Jesus went into the desert where he fasted for forty days and forty nights.

Spending time in a remote place is a way of blocking out worldly affairs, allowing uninterrupted time to concentrate on growing closer to God. We may not be able to go off to an isolated place for forty days, but we could try to focus our thoughts more on God during Lent.

Whatever we decide to do during Lent, we could try not to get so involved in what we are doing as to forget why we are doing it. We could try to follow the example of Jesus and use our forty days as a time for drawing closer to God.

Lent

Temptation

During the forty days of Lent, we're reminded that Jesus went into the desert for forty days, where he was tempted to turn stones into bread; to prove how great he was, and where he was tempted with worldly goods. Despite his hunger, he didn't dwell on the thought of bread; nor did he dwell on how he could prove his greatness; nor did he dwell on the splendour of the worldly goods he was shown. Instead, he focused on God.

We are tempted many times, every day. We are tempted to think ill of others; to lose patience with others; to be selfish and not share what we have with others. Unlike Jesus, we tend to dwell on the temptation. If we start to think ill of someone, or feel impatient, or selfish, we tend to think of all the reasons why we are justified in thinking these thoughts, telling ourselves that we're right to think this way.

Instead, we should follow the example of Jesus. When we start to think unkind or selfish thoughts, we should immediately turn our thoughts to God, dwelling on his goodness towards us and his wish that we love our neighbours.

Lent

Prayer

Silence is golden. In today's busy world, with its incessant noise, this certainly is true. In order to communicate with God we need silence.

Matthew 14:23 (and Mark 6:46) tells us that Jesus went up on a mountainside by himself to pray. Mark 1:35 says that very early in the morning, while it was still dark, Jesus got up, left the house and went off to a solitary place where he prayed. If Jesus needed solitude to pray, we surely need it. We don't have to go up a mountainside; we can use any unoccupied room in our home. We can decide on a time in the day when we know we'll not be interrupted for ten minutes.

We need quiet to let inner silence grow so that inner life might flourish. Just as we need to constantly clear the weeds from our garden to make space for the flowers to grow, so we need to regularly clear the distractions within ourselves to make space for God's words.

Lent may be a good time to start the habit of daily prayer, so book yourself a time and place and enjoy some golden moments.

Mothering Sunday

The mother of Jesus is mentioned twice in John's Gospel. Chapter 2 tells of a wedding at Cana to which Jesus, his mother and his disciples were invited. The wedding feast was very important, maybe going on for a week, and to fail in proper hospitality was a serious offence. Mary told Jesus that they had run out of wine, but he replied that his time had not yet come. His mother, however, told the servants to do whatever he tells them and, as we know, he saved the day. This brief description shows how Mary was sensitive to the dire circumstances of her hosts and how Jesus, a man of around thirty, in the company of his friends, was, nevertheless, sensitive to his mother's concerns.

John 19:27 describes how, when suffering an agonising death on the cross, Jesus entrusted the care of his mother to his favourite disciple.

The few details of these two events paint pictures of a thoughtful woman who cared about others and a son who, despite his important mission, showed great respect and concern for his mother. Two good role models to think about on Mothering Sunday.

Palm Sunday

On Palm Sunday Christians celebrate the day that Jesus rode into Jerusalem on a colt and the crowds greeted him with palm branches, crying 'Hosanna', which means 'Save now' (Matthew 21:1; Mark 11:1; John 12:12). The crowds expected him to save them by driving the Romans out of Palestine. People of importance would ride in a chariot or at least on horseback, so by riding on a colt Jesus demonstrated his humility. This showed that he was not a political saviour, but a spiritual saviour and the way of spiritual salvation is through humility.

A few days later, at the Last Supper, he gave a further display of humility when he washed his disciples feet (John 13:1), a menial task normally performed by a servant. Jesus explained to them that he, who they called 'Lord' and 'Teacher', had done this in order to set an example; as he had done for them, so they should do for each other.

These are two good lessons to reflect on whenever we feel tempted towards self-importance.

Maundy Thursday

'Peace I leave with you; my peace I give you,' said Jesus to his disciples during the Last Supper (John 14:27). But how do we find this peace? The followers of St. Benedict believe that there is no peace without sacrifice and therefore their symbol is the Latin word for peace 'pax' surrounded by a crown of thorns.

The sacrifice we make is in the way we live our daily lives. It involves giving up our selfish attitude, giving up putting ourselves first and instead putting others before ourselves. But we often feel too busy to even think about others. In that case, we need to reflect on what makes us so busy. It's very easy to fall into the trap of being busy with the wrong things. The desire for the bigger car; the better holiday, or higher status can drive us to overwork. If we get caught up in this cycle, we have to decide whether or not to sacrifice some of our ambitions.

It's our choice as to how busy we are. If we choose to fill our life with the right things, then we will find the promised peace.

Good Friday

As Jesus was crucified he said, 'Father, forgive them, because they do not know what they are doing,' (Luke 23:34).

It has been said that when Luke's Gospel was being copied many scribes omitted this line because they found it too difficult to believe that Jesus would forgive even his executioners.

Also in Luke's Gospel (23:39) it says that while one of the criminals hanging beside Jesus spoke irreverently to him, the other defended Jesus and Jesus told him that he would, that day, join him in paradise. This criminal, at the point of death, was offered forgiveness.

These two incidents show the infinite love and forgiveness of God. No matter what we have done, there is nothing God will not forgive, and it is never too late to repent. Likewise, we must follow the example of Jesus and learn to be forgiving. God is the source of compassion and the closer we live to the heart of God, the more compassion will flow through our own heart, just like Jesus.

Easter Day

In a letter written about 30 years after the crucifixion of Jesus, Peter the apostle, wrote that Jesus died 'so that we might die to sins and live for righteousness' (1 Peter 2:24).

If we want to 'die to sins' we have to kill off our old ways, such as our selfishness, our impatience, our greed, our vanity. But killing off our old ways is extremely difficult, because it means changing our ways and none of us likes change. We feel secure in our old familiar ways and we can feel threatened by any sort of change. So, we make excuses and think of reasons why we shouldn't change. Making changes can cause us a lot of suffering, because parts of us are dying. But allowing the old self to die is the only way the new self can come alive.

At Eastertide we think about the suffering of Jesus on his way to Calvary, his death on the cross and his resurrection to new life. We too have to make a painful journey as we shed our old ways and eventually die to sins, before we can start to live a new and righteous life.

Pentecost

Examples of the misery caused by separation and the joy that unity brings can be seen around all the time.

The Story of Babel (Genesis 11) tells of separation when people could not understand each other and they were scattered over the face of the earth.

The events of Pentecost (Acts 2:2) are seen as a reversal of this when people of every nationality could understand perfectly what the apostles were telling them and about three thousand people joined the apostles that day.

Separation of any kind, sometimes caused by misunderstanding, can bring misery, whereas unity brings joy. The events of Pentecost show that the Spirit of God takes away all divisions and brings the intoxicating joy of unity.

If we, for any reason, have become separated from someone we care about, perhaps we should try to reverse the situation and seek the joy of unity.

Ascension Day

On Ascension Day Christians are reminded of the last commission that Jesus gave to his disciples: 'Go out to the whole world' (Mark 16:15). He wanted them to befriend everyone they met, without exception. He didn't want them to be inward-looking. He didn't want them to settle down and close in on themselves.

We're all tempted to form our own little groups, because that makes us feel safe. But Jesus didn't stay in a safe place – he went out.

Also, Jesus was inclusive. He mixed with a variety of people, not just with his own kind. Women were ignored in public and Samaritans hated, but Jesus spoke to a woman at Jacob's well (John 4:7) who was not only a Samaritan, but also a woman of ill-repute – yet he spoke to her as an equal. He dealt with people from all walks of life – from a leper to a centurion; from a friend's mother-in-law to an official's daughter, along with tax collectors, sinners (Matthew 8-9) and many more.

We can go out and make the world a better place by befriending everyone we meet, without exception, and treating them as an equal.

Guy Fawkes Night

On Guy Fawkes night many of us will watch firework displays. Amid 'oohs' and 'ahhs' we'll delight in the whistling, crackling and banging as comets rise and burst into glittering starbursts. But we'll also witness an example of how short-lived some things are; each firework lasts only a few seconds. Most things last longer than fireworks, but nothing lasts forever. Looks fade; careers end; goods get lost, broken or stolen.

Jesus urges us not to store up treasures on earth where moth and rust destroy and where thieves break in and steal, but to store up for ourselves treasures in heaven, for where our treasure is, there our heart will be also (Matthew 6:19).

Our heart, or mind, is preoccupied with what we hold to be most valuable. Therefore we must ensure that what we treasure is spiritual and imperishable and not those things which deteriorate and are in continuous danger of being stolen or destroyed.

There's nothing wrong with owning things. But when those things become our greatest treasure, we're heading for a fall, because we'll eventually lose them. However, when the most important thing in our life is our right relationship with God and our fellow man, we possess a lasting treasure.

Remembrance Day

Let Them be One

On the first Christmas Day of World War I in 1914 a truce began when the soldiers started to sing Christmas carols. Gradually both sets of soldiers moved out of their trenches to meet in no-man's land and after exchanging stories and gifts, they played football together.

Those who can remember the years during World War II will tell us that, despite the horror of it all, an enduring memory is the wonderful feeling of unity, of all pulling together for the common good, of neighbours caring about neighbours, of strangers helping strangers, and the many strong friendships forged with people they would otherwise treat with hostility and suspicion.

These war stories are examples of man's innate desire to be connected with his fellow man.

In the final prayer of Jesus before he was taken away to die, he repeatedly prayed for unity, 'Let them be one' (John 17:11,21,22,23).

As we discard our poppies for another year, let us replace them with the prayer of Jesus firmly lodged in our hearts, lest we forget.

Remembrance Day

Lay Down His Life

'Greater love has no-one than this, that he lay down his life for his friends' (John 15:13). This is part of the last discourse given by Jesus to his disciples before he lay down his life. It is a quote that is brought to mind on Remembrance Day.

On Remembrance Day we honour those men and women who lay down their life, not just for friends, but for strangers. They did this in the hope of making the world a better place in which to live.

Most of us are not asked to lay down our life, but what we can do is try to lay aside our petty self-centredness in order to make the world a better place in which to live.

If we can remember every day to lay aside our self-centredness by trying to be more understanding of others, more compassionate, more caring, more patient, more respectful of other people's views, and try to do acts of kindness whenever we can, we will be making the world a better place, and making worthwhile the sacrifice of those who lay down their life for us.

BBC's Children In Need

The BBC's Children In Need must be the most popular charity event of the year. Perhaps this is because we all recognise the vulnerability of children; their total trust in us as their only hope; their complete dependence on us to help them. They have not yet become cynical, suspicious, or able to look after themselves.

In Matthew 18:3 Jesus says 'Unless you change and become like little children, you will never enter the kingdom of heaven.'

Jesus is asking us to reverse our belief that we don't need God to look after us; to turn our disbelief in God's goodness into belief; to swap our suspicion for total trust; to become completely dependent on God to help us in every aspect of our lives.

God knows our needs better than we know them ourselves. All we have to do is put aside our arrogance; to approach God with the vulnerability of a child, totally trusting in his love for us – to turn to God as his children in need.

Index

1 Corinthians 11:6 37
1 Corinthians 13 48
1 Corinthians 13:11 75
1 John 4:16 26
1 Kings 19:11 27
1 Kings 3 29
1 Timothy 4:16 58
2 Corinthians 12:12 58
2 Corinthians 3:1 74
2 Peter 1:6 58
2 Thessalonians 1:4,3:5 .. 58
Acts 2 93
Acts 2:2 110
Aesop
   The Wind And The Sun
   27
Atkins, Margaret 33
Cope, Wendy
   30th December 91
Dickens, Charles
   A Christmas Carol 89
   A Tale of Two Cities .. 47
   David Copperfield 36
   Great Expectations 84
Eliot, George
   Middlemarch 75
Esther 34
Fiennes, Sir Ranulph 45
Genesis 74

Genesis 1 30
Genesis 1:11 15
Genesis 11 110
Genesis 12-22 23
Genesis 2 63
Gormley, Antony
   Another Place 41
Guest, Edgar 61
Häring, Bernard 26
Hebrews 10:36, 12:1 58
Holman Hunt, William 88
Isaiah 53 66
James 1:12 58
Job 11
John 1:46 37
John 10 80
John 10:10 46
John 12:12 106
John 13:1 106
John 13:34 .... 37, 49
John 13:35 .... 62, 96
John 14:27 107
John 14:6 51
John 15:12 37
John 15:12,17 49
John 15:13 114
John 17 83
John 17:11,21,22,23 113
John 19:11 55

John 19:27 105	Luke 6:29 37
John 2 105	Luke 6:41 39
John 20:24 12	Luke 8:1 35
John 21:16 81	Luke 8:15 58
John 4:7 111	Luke 8:21 91
John 6:1 ....72, 82	Luke 9:10 .... 72, 82
John 6:16 24	Luke 9:23 20
John 8:12 ....44, 88	Luke 9:24 47
Jonah 86	Mandeville, Bernard de
Judges 12........................83	The Fable of the Bees 33
Judith...............................52	Mark 1:12........................ 79
Luke 10:21......................84	Mark 1:15...................... 101
Luke 10:25......................54	Mark 1:35...................... 104
Luke 10:27......................37	Mark 10:17...................... 14
Luke 10:38......................64	Mark 10:46...................... 12
Luke 12:15......................33	Mark 11:1...................... 106
Luke 12:22......................85	Mark 12:14...................... 90
Luke 12:31......................70	Mark 12:30...................... 37
Luke 13:10......................74	Mark 14:27...................... 81
Luke 15:11..........22, 28, 38	Mark 14:30...................... 93
Luke 15:7........................83	Mark 14:72...................... 81
Luke 17:11......................32	Mark 16:15.................... 111
Luke 17:21......................41	Mark 2:22........................ 92
Luke 17:3........................87	Mark 3:33........................ 91
Luke 18:18......................14	Mark 4:1 35
Luke 18:9........................17	Mark 4:35........................ 27
Luke 19:12......................78	Mark 6:32.................. 72, 82
Luke 2..............................90	Mark 6:45........................ 24
Luke 20:21......................90	Mark 6:46...................... 104
Luke 23:34....................108	Mark 8:34........................ 20
Luke 23:39....................108	Mark 8:35........................ 47
Luke 24:13......................13	Matthew 11:25 84
Luke 4:1..........................79	Matthew 11:28 65
Luke 5:37........................92	Matthew 12:1 74
Luke 6:27..................37, 50	Matthew 12:48 91

Matthew 13:1 35
Matthew 14:13 .... 72, 82
Matthew 14:22 24
Matthew 14:23 104
Matthew 16:24 20
Matthew 16:25 47
Matthew 18:15 .... 18, 87
Matthew 18:21 87
Matthew 18:22 37
Matthew 18:23 25
Matthew 18:3 115
Matthew 19:16 14
Matthew 19:19 37
Matthew 2 90
Matthew 20:1 77
Matthew 21:1 106
Matthew 22:16 90
Matthew 22:21 53
Matthew 22:37 37
Matthew 23:12 36
Matthew 25:14 78
Matthew 25:35 13
Matthew 25:40 16
Matthew 26:31 81
Matthew 26:34 93
Matthew 26:75 81
Matthew 28:20 37
Matthew 4:1 79
Matthew 5:13 31

Matthew 5:3 59
Matthew 5:40 67
Matthew 5:43 37
Matthew 5:44 50
Matthew 5:8 73
Matthew 5:9 57
Matthew 6:19 112
Matthew 6:25 37
Matthew 6:26 85
Matthew 6:33 70
Matthew 6:5 60
Matthew 7:13 68
Matthew 7:21 45
Matthew 7:3 39
Matthew 7:7 69
Matthew 8-9 111
Matthew 9:17 92
My Fair Lady 19
Newman, John Henry .. 42
Revelation 74
Revelation 3:20 88
Romans 5:3 58
Ruth 71
Shakespeare, William
   Othello 38
   The Winter's Tale 21
St Francis of Assisi 61
Widdecombe, Ann 60

Printed in Great Britain
by Amazon